CSU Poetry Series LXVIII

Cleveland State University Poetry Center

ACKNOWLEDGMENTS

Grateful acknowledgments to the editors of the following journals, in which these poems first appeared: *Georgia Review*: "With Crickets"; *Virginia Quarterly Review*: "Petersburg Dawn"; *Black Warrior Review*: "Sunflower-Brother," "Listening Room"; *New Millenium Writings*: "Late Summer Fever"; *Puerto del Sol*: "Aubade in Blue"; *Quarterly West*: "Bible Burning"; *Spoon River Poetry Anthology*: "Self-Portrait in a Dead Possum's Eye"; *Poetry West*: "Eclipse"; *Louisiana Literature*: "Elegy of a Living Man," "Pastoral," "Fireflies"; *American Poetry Review*: "Depression Glass"; *Great River Review*: "Depression Glass," "Jerusalem"; *Coe Review*: "Elegy with Small-Mouth Bass"; *Pleiades*: "Black Pony on a Bank of the James," "New River Blues," "Skin," "The Cold War," "The Kiss.

"Late Summer Fever" was the winner of the 1999 New Millenium Poetry Award; the second section of this book was awarded the 2005 Dana Award in Poetry; and "Depression Glass" won the 2001 *American Literary Review* Poetry Prize.

I would also like to thank the Cleveland State University Poetry Center and all of the people who work there, especially Susan Grimm and Rita Grabowski.

Impossible without my family and friends, that catalogue of ships too expansive to number here.

ISBN: 978-1-880834-74-9
Library of Congress Catalog Card Number: 2006937813

Ohio Arts Council
A STATE AGENCY
THAT SUPPORTS PUBLIC
PROGRAMS IN THE ARTS

ζ

SUNFLOWER
BROTHER

ξ

by Sam Witt

Holms -
So great to meet you
and hang out. I'd love
to correspond and get to
know your work (and you)
even better. Please remember
to submit to our anthology
Boston, MA
March 2013

ζ

SUNFLOWER
BROTHER

ξ

CONTENTS

Three

FOR GRAVES TRUESDALE, IN LOVING MEMORY, 1963-1994

AND FOR RICHARD SPOTTSWOOD CLAY WITT

Ah! Sunflower! weary of time.
Who countest the steps of the Sun,
Seeking after that sweet golden clime
Where the traveller's journey is done.

Where the Youth pined away with desire,
And the pale Virgin shrouded in snow:
Arise from their graves and aspire,
Where my Sun-flower wishes to go.

William Blake, "Ah! Sunflower"

THE COLD WAR

A field of razorwire
drifting through my sleep, a chip of potassium
glowing faintly under my fingernail,
I swear it was my own

little war, the terrified world
spinning like a coin—
and I could never find the finger to touch your face,
by accident, in a filling station.

For instance, two boys catch
a hummingbird out of the living air.
They seal it in a jar without holes, its flecked,
metallic wings tremble, flutter still.

I watched it just now, spinning
to a stop, this dwarfed planet breaking down.
I suppose I am an instant, a cooling tower
of concealed clouds. We were that close.

From a thousand miles away
you burn a valley of flammable air
into my chest, and I breathe it, when I sleep.
In school they taught us

each atom was a solar system,
with a sun, and thousands of planets.
They were wrong. They were wrong
about my finger,

capable of touching your cheek.

One

A BRIEF HISTORY OF THE SOUTH

for Emmett Till, July 25, 1944 - August 28, 1955

Night air. Sweetgum and oak; the stain
of Sunday greens, all the life boiled out.
Once again the fields are virginal,
gauzed in mist. A whippoorwill sings high

in the cottonwood, sings absurdly;
the Tallahatchie, a lead angel
that rises and falls back in its chains,
keeps sliding nowhere to the color of rust.

Why are the trees cloaked in black?
Heaped with a requisite sorrow, like
the attics of the dead, sheeted, emptied out:
dust, ash, the shadows of the world—

the moon has swung to a stop.
Like a brass clockweight it holds down the sky.
And why are the stars cloaked in black,
expectant, only the tips flashing?

Because his eyes continue to fill
with a wild darkness: a last song whistles
through his teeth, falls still. Because there's no air
in a river, and a body to breath it,

his lungs are filled.
O Father, O Holy Bruise.

Afterwards they chained an old gin fan
to his neck. Arms, chest, fingers,
into the river's dark love: a mouthful of dogtags,
silt. The blood. The wine.

PETERSBURG DAWN

Seconds before the explosion,
crickets were chewing the thirsty air with their legs,

thousands of them together: the air screamed.
Silence. A spark

could've touched the grass off.

He was thinking
of mother's forehead, furrowing slightly

as the bullet buried itself with a thud
in the temple of Chestnut, his childhood horse.

He must have believed the crickets

would put even *them* to sleep,
four gauzy cottonfields away:

against a leaning ash tree, half-cocked over his gun,
he fell asleep.

Seconds before the tunnelled earth
flashed below him,

seconds before the sun broke its chains,

he was back in the barn again,
hunched into the hammock, gathered into his own arms;

each crumbled tobacco mote was drifting,
suddenly alive in the swallow smothered loft.

A moth lit on his shoulder.

Exploded into his ear,
and father jerked him up by the wrist—

think of family Bible leather, cracked, unkind—
he woke alone,

"Isaac, Isaac,"
the sweating leaves burst into ash

where they found his father's voice.
Hardly had the tents become lanterns

when the air was snatched
of him: feel your lungs expanding now, collapsing.

Hear it with him,
the first four notes of grandfather's watch

chiming the quarter hour before they snapped,
roared into an ocean in his torn ear.

Just between us, the air kissed itself.

Kissed his entire body in sudden daylight,
a public gesture somehow made secret,

a sheet of honey soaking his woollen pants,
molding the coins in his pocket into a silver lump.

Now that he's lifted by a monstrous falling
from under this scorched wing,

we can feel his incandescence, wet, heavy hay
falling forever; at his body's insistence,

we must believe the rain evaporates
as it broke, lifting the smell of burning horse:

Lord, Lord, they are all free now.

TURN OF THE CENTURY

The traditional, garlanded flowers—tigerlily,
blunt rose—the ones that fill her toy-sized casket,
have been pollinated a little early this season,
just like her swollen cheeks, onto which
the slightest scent of fallen pears has settled
beside the place where the parlor's cracked Bible
blurs away at the photo's edge,
where the albumenized paper curls into the dark air
that might still be filling
her deflated lungs, even now,
could those small bellows
have only worked up one more breath,
and disturbed a century of silver dust.

Six feet away from the tripod, the dark cloth
thrown in a hood over your head,
in sharply creased, heavy linen she lies,
perfected, arranged, not really a toddler anymore,
her powdered eyelids half-closed.
Like theater curtains, or skin, they reveal a milky stage
where her father leans against the broken piano,
a dull reflection in the dull, translucid fat
of her eyes. Those eyelids will not close,
no matter how many weeks dysentery—
or was it flu—kneaded this man's daughter,
leaving her cold, no matter how hard you stare
through the cloaked camera's heavily warping lens
until your eyes throb. The coins,
the ones in your left pocket—does it occur to you?—
once weighted those stubborn lids.

Now her father's shifting, one foot to the other,
a cloth hat twisted in both soil-caked hands.
Keep still, you think. But instead impatience, or mercy,
stirs your trigger finger,

and you lift the shutter early, trip the bulb.
Just then in the sideyard, cousin Luke
releases a pigeon from its cage; strapped
to one leg, a message of quarantine, early death:
with a sulfur flash, the window freezes into gray shadow:
her tiny, sculpted features
demand the parlor light, that the pigeon
continue its long climb forever in a speck of gray,
demand that her father's face surrender to the corner shades
and be hidden in a sudden white blur
for a century, or more.

WITH CRICKETS

for Victoria Helen Johnson, 1958-

It could have been on a night like this,
with crickets and rain,
when the swallows and the wrens
have sounded their last wing-flaps
through the branches, have taken roost.
I could feel the crickets like a fever on the air,
their last, dumb song maddening, alive:
you are standing again in that spring of honeysuckle
and oak, in a garden, your stomach barely swollen.
Of all this, though, what matters is *here*:
two camel crickets, after the rain has stopped,
mating on my window sill, one on top
of the other, abdomens splotched
and spangled as a lizard's back.

I can't believe how still they are.
One antenna tentative and sweeping, how slowly
they turn towards me, opening,
pulsing now, stirring the dried shell
of a yellow jacket. When one leg lifts
and rubs across another, I'm holding my breath.
Then, at last, the warbling call cracks,
draws itself out, a single breath
in my room. I put out the light, lie back,
I slowly draw one leg across the other.
When a human embryo is seven weeks old,
the brain shines through its forehead, a cloud
of light, belly-deep and breathing,
the whole, luminous mass cabled and alone,

as the moon, torn off new, must have been,
cooling in its black waters. When I heard
what you did to yourself, the cyanide
on the fruit roll-up, the easy chair reclined,
I could hardly see your face. I had never

even touched you—a night like this one,
with rain, and crickets, your eyes cracked open,
still. If I could build a boat
with these words, and float back, I'd drift
on a sure tide, back over the depth
of your last living room. I'd stretch my arm down
into that still black and connect
for a moment, my body filling with light,

slowly, the way an oak draws water.

ELEGY WITH SMALL-MOUTH BASS

for Ann Johnson

A shift in the sluggish poplars
and snow clouds the belly of the iced-up pond.
The snow has been asleep in the boughs for almost six months.
Six months since you found your daughter there, reclined in the easy
    chair.
Six months since the green light entered her eyes for the last time,
the way sunlight enters the leaf.
Her body was discolored,
but it's winter now, and everything keeps talking to itself,
a dry click as ice-cased leaves lift and fall; the hawthorne,
with its ciliac snow clusters newly blossomed, explodes
into blackbirds when you aim your flashlight
into the understory, a sudden hot flash
in your face and upper body
and your heart begins to race . . .

There were too many bass in the pond last summer.
The water brimmed and pulsed with their small bodies.
They jumped clear, fell, slid back. They snapped their tails,
whipped up the silt, and burrowed deep into the mud
to feed on frogspawn,
                  but everything keeps talking to itself now:
a murmur in the frozen stalks,
ice-particles, entering the inverted trees of your chest:
even at the bottom of the pond
the bass keep opening and closing their mouths a little
as they wait with slowed hearts in their shrouds of silt.

Think of it, how the water
would not stop boiling, how it tossed gently
like a body turning out of sleep.
How you still sometimes dream up her body
as it must have been, breathing out its last silver noise,
a pure cloud that burns faintly, then dissolves,
with its many frozen voices through the frozen weeds.

PASTORAL

Perhaps in the spider's dream
a swallow's egg rests in her gentle, lifeless hand.
Perhaps, just now, a blue-green hummingbird
has darted swiftly between the forefinger
and the steaming thumb, and sips a nervous meal,

perhaps, through that cracked, oozing shell—

In this birch ravine her body lies for keeps.
Silver leaves fall onto the packed soil and become
nothing more than leaves. The fallen trunks lie on their sides
yet can't quite seem to crumble into soil:

into their forked, spiny branches
sunlight has softly let drop its threadbare linen,

has scattered a delicate ground ash
over the sackcloth bark. Why should the sunlight care?
Why should the tall vigil of those leaning birches,

changing light to sugar,
drawing it deep within those straight, white ribs,
have any eyes for this? Or the wakened spider—

black tooth, glass strand thin as drool—
continue to spread a wasted lace

over the pale skin of her ribcage so tightly locked?
A waterdrop falls, piercing without hatred
the thin, blue hymen of her eye, where the boys are already reflected,
the ones who won't find her for a day, where an albino deer

overlooks her as it noses the leaves: neck and leg,

rippling, milk-white shank, warped and reflected
in the muted lens of the lightbulb, which blooms
like a baby's fist from her mouth. Perhaps her body—bark-stripped,
one streaked arm hiding a breast—has it already blended
into the naked shapes of fallen birch?

MORNING WEB

I.

Splinted stalks
rattle and lean, drawn inward by the threads
of this spider's web.
They listen
like old men, desiccated to an electric whisper:
her soft net, after all,
a sort of love, a soft embrace, messages circling
to its center—
prey, fattened like sheep
on a hillside; a bumblebee, half-spun, still pulsing
in its deathsweater,
a tiny leaf
suspended, and dewdrops, drawn out along
her trembling, steel lace
that dissolves into music circling inward,
where the music is then picked clean,
a low voltage of sunlight
touching her sleep—tiny surgeon, saint,
awaken into the ecstacy of human breath;
begin to stitch now. Turn the sleeping bee
until it shines,
like crystal, until the entire web jumps
to an unheard music:
and the pollen sifts down,
like yellow rosin, until a moth catches,
unsnags itself, rises, bitter angel,
and it's snared once more:
dangle it down, mother, spin it from a honeythread
the way a circus lady is spun,
by the teeth—

2.

A year ago yesterday
they shot Ceauscescu and his wife. A quick scene,

really, some stuttered words *pause,*
the bodies falling
and falling like acrobats in replay, *back and forth,*
back and forth. He looked so weak—twisted legs,
chest full of straw—I thought his face
was going to dissolve, though it took both hands
for the guard to lift his head to the camera.
And it was only yesterday,
in the same part of the world,
that thirty-seven old people were shot
as they waited in line for bread.
                                    I watched the screen
as a boy watches an aquarium: human larvae,
spun into a hunch by the camera's shaking grain
cut a face of rags tightly bound *pan in, pan in*
the old teeth blackened and worn.
But now I'm looking into a photograph, taken last year
in Gary, Indiana, the foreground an angry blur
that focuses itelf into a gun some father holds.
Now a boy breaks stride in the doorway, naked;
now held in orbit by the blunt shape of his dad,
exposed by the sweep of an arclight
from a police helicopter above: this blurring form
will drain the scene for years to come,
the way sirens drain the slums.

3.
                    This morning
the morning is too clear, spun down
to a fine web
                    between the inwardly leaning, desiccated stalks.
Overhead, a sunflower explodes to the grain-gold
            of a lion's face,
then burns back down to black seed and husk;
odor of a bloodrose:

17

the spider sleeps.
And in each of her dewdrops, a little world
about to fall—
                    irises, weighted under by fistfuls of the sun;
clouds, hanging on the blue filament
        like cocoons; birds,
scattered like poppyseed: *yesterday, yesterday*
a muffled applause . . .

MAN IN A GLADE

A step down, & I'm knee-deep in weeds.
One foot planted firmly, the other flexed & lifting
over the bolted ribbon of the guardrail—

Then a rough, green breath,
sheen of shadow & dew, clumps of grass
stretching away in swirls at the trunks of pines,
a few blades carefully drawn through
the rusted holes of a tin can.
& all before me, the loose rubble
thrown by cars—exhaust pipe,
a stiffened bluejay with splayed wings,
a torn rubber half-swallowed in grass.
I slide down the cluttered, broken hillside,
my tie loosening, my pants soaked to the knees
in green juice & clay, I'm lashed hard
by the young branches,
the burning chemicals of sap.
                                        Here,
where the embankment has levelled off,
here before the river,
where the trees open into sunlight, and the grass
has been swept back, yellow at the roots,
I lean like a sapling.
Thrashing darkly in its deciduous growth, kudzu & oak,
the other side of the river has dropped its low branching
over the flashflood-scooped bank,
a long drag across the dark surface.
                                        & the river—
It carries itself into those washed-out hollows,
the soaked cavities gorged with leaf rot. The surface
swallows my reflection, alternating between the empty, blue sky
& me:
corrugated & glassy, the surface spits my reflection back out,
a brown shimmer of bottles numbing each ankle: water,

19

humming quietly in its plaits: dirty,
wandering charges that bump against my thighs—
water is the spilled braid,
the invisible fishstring through their gills;
water, their slow breath, a prickle & slide of scale
as I wade in to my waist.
One of them floats up from the pool,
sleepy from her long, muted channel, drowsed, stunned,
as she surfaces through the broken rainbow-scrim of oil,
having risen through the polluted depths
& just barely awakened in my hands.
Her unclosable eyes are somehow too clear to hold the reflection
of my emptying, human form in true depth,
though they do, on the rounded surface, if I tilt her just right.
How strange to hold her,
just under the surface! How strange to lift her out of the water
& hold her there, just above the water's troubled skin,
& to watch her, gulping that poisonous air!
Diodes of light glister the scales; huge, distended pupils,
suddenly somehow empty when I shift her,
as if my image had been swallowed by a clear, black film,
then her mouth, opening & clothing the air
with each drowsed emission of what should be water,
exhausted in its own silvery, oxidized mask:
a silvery quick, the blue flick of her tail,
suddenly come alive
as it conducts a new current, flashing the light
against the back of my hand, up, for a millisecond, she slips,
then capsized, flapping airborne
for just a second into the gasping air.

SELF-PORTRAIT IN A DEAD POSSUM'S EYE

One eye cleaned out
like a wall-socket, unplugged.
The other intact, staring up at me. The two of us
breathing that same, hungry calm,
the same light those kudzu leaves are panting
like tongues: in this place,

where foxes drive their hissing prey
under the wheels of trains, where possums like you
would rather bow to the pressures
of a steel sky than be torn:
where bitch-possums like you lie down
in the oily water between slats

and play dead, and die,
and split open like swollen pods,
bearing all thirteen lucky teats when the feathered seeds of milkweed drift:
in the tiny place of this missing eye,
time winks in a spark of the sun, like a dime, spinning to a stop.
Above me, a murder of crows, assembled on the wires.

At my feet, a murder of flies.
I have been told that dying
is a kind of honey that soaks us from inside.
I hunker and touch a miniature thigh: my finger burns a little.
I hear flies, hatching in this distended ear,
bronze and blue and green, like darting spores,

flies singing Dixie as my lips move.
I lift the Confederacy on the tip of my middle finger.
I'm a boy again, holding my sliced finger
above a plastic tub. The circle of water
is deep with my blood. It's dusk,
it's my own distorted face,

flashing once in astonished light:
raised cheekbones, edges of silver
unearthed in a field; a stunned, prehensile smile.
I am my own finger now, nothing more;
this is the way I'm lifted
I am smoldering like a cotton field,

this is the way the blood falls,
exploding into the water as each drop disappears
into that missing eye with each misfired second,
with each spark of *me* that falls. A long hiss
disturbs the mangy hillside as I stare
through your barbed, razory teeth,

passing through the grass,
down the bank, away.
I have been staring into this blue gaze
for a day. What is it I touched,
bursting again in your eye? *Don't ask.*
Dusk-blood, aglow in the kudzu's thick palms?

A scrap of pure rage? The fox
that drove you here to stay?

Carry it in you like a fire.
Breather, walk away.

ECLIPSE

Then a hint of cold drifting
through the window panes of the classroom, its honey
aching in the back of my head, in the light
that had been floating through my eyes in a slant, all afternoon,
a cold hush spreading into the plaster specks, into fingers,
stitches of chalk, the words on the blackboard
suddenly grown strange.

So they led us, class after class,
children in furrows, down the long, vaulted stairwell
into the courtyard. I can still feel
the light growing sharp, shedding itself.
I can still taste a shadow of fire, that afternoon
the sky flickered, and the air went numb,
and shed us into our small bodies, cold.

Our teachers told us, "This is the sun going out."
"Don't look up, it'll burn your eyes away, you could go blind."
But we'd stared into it before, those nights
mom and dad darkened together in the bedroom's eye,
one on top of the other, *We just couldn't stop.*
And then the doorway light blowing out, the leaves
casting tiny crescent shadows of light on the pavement
as the retina scar went trailing off . . .

And if it is fire, cold fire we end in after all,
a newly divided light we could only glimpse
in that sharp angle of cold?
Then, as in the dream, only the fire will sound,
so deeply I feel it in my gut. And if the unborn children
are there, rowing off into the waters? A small scar
will heal as it trails the boat into a blinded sun,
into God's thumbprint, a scar I can't follow home.

No breath, not so much as a flapping wing.

Only the sound of the creek
swallowing itself. What I remember is the streetlamps,
warming up, then fading,
to a full-body immersion that left us cold.
Black water, black fire—could we only enter you,
and cross back over cold—fatherless now, hunched like children,
Our traveling garments forgotten and reassumed like skin.

SKIN

Forget the star-riddled saint,
his shut eyelids, the drifting countries of his skin.
Forget the tiny quills which still sing in the spine:
ten fingers, ten little flesh-kisses,

your hands will betray you, and touch
the burning wings of Henry Johnson's prize swan,
whose throat he slit, just before he hanged himself
as his father did, a century before, in the barn.

Just before your hands
floated a moment in those astonished eyes,
as they do now, and reached out blind,
and forgot our fathers' deeds.

The ones we wear on our backs, like skin.

Two

SEIZURE

You wait for it to come,
breath held, you stand at the window,
the air burying itself in handfuls in the trees, swell after swell.
All day long you feel it pulse in your stomach.

And the dining room filled with voices, pitch
after pitch, mixing into the hot crack
of bourbon over ice. I remember lying
in a darkened room, my brother beside me,
breathing, as the night went thick with sirens, drained,
and the house deadened,
a still across water.
              After the storm,
the air is almost clear—slabs of concrete
lifted out of the sidewalk, opened, the trees
sunk into houses, cable and splinter, streetlamps
scattered across the asphalt, mounds of clay
shorn from the banks.

We lowered ourselves down into the cavity,
root by pried root, the pipes snapped, wrenched free,
felt the cold steam settling around us, everything glazed.
And a bird whistling overhead.

I saw my father laid out on a stretcher once.
They heaved him up, a man on each limb,
they laid him out, the way a steer is held before slaughter,
each vein on his neck drawn into relief,
pulled the long canvas straps over his chest and stomach
until the steel spindles bowed.

But in the church, his voice rises like water:
trembling in cadence, thick, it resounds
through the pews worn smooth, up the wall, staining
the plaster, the windows. It strings

the crucifix and the altar with its dark weed, his voice
straining, roaring like the sea in winter.

The bull keeps coming back, mounted on a crest
of water. The neighborhood slowly breathes
its muted candlelight:

These are the psalms you have been given:
These, the last breaths.

STEPPING INTO THE LIGHT

for Clay Crenshaw, 1900-1986.

Now that the morning has broken its veils
into dew, a low mist dropped at the base of the pylons;
    now that the apple blossoms are half-opened
    around me, sugary and blind, half-sealed
        with their own black juices;

        now that this valley
has unfolded below—electric fencing, meadows, sheep—
    I stand here at the edge of an orchard in mid-spring,
    I've driven out from the city, alone.
        Tiny in its dropcloth of fog,

    my friend's farm sleeps: his trees
are heavy with dawn. Someone who loved them hangs from a hook
    inside. Someone who stands here, alone,
    and breathes the murderous odor

        of apple blossoms and wet hay—

Although the old house didn't smell of apples or sheep, the cracked odor
of that hallway has crept into my nose just now, a dull flash of sunlight on
split pine. Something, perhaps, in the way the clock ticked at nightfall,
striking each quarter hour as the window panes grew darker, the clock's
ghostly, oval face like a moon over the oily waters of a harbor in fall, beside
the heating vent, where I warmed a petri dish of sheep's blood near the
front door one winter, until it grew long, blond hairs. Something in the
crumbled plaster, the wet light of his jaundiced room, where I wandered as
a child. I start with the ceiling cracks, running into each other like rivers
on an old map. I follow them down to the yellowed wallpaper, which hangs
from its watermarked corner like skin.

Then the mirror, with its tiny, dark-haired boy, lost in a silver cloud of
tarnish and flecked paint. Then the chest of drawers—gold cufflinks, a
wooden box, an empty glass. Where is that small girl who cleaned his room
once a week, lifting those emptied bottles and setting them back

down into a brown paper bag, here, where he slept, pulled out across these sheets, drifting? Where are the two porcelain dolls I found one afternoon, thirty years later, the ones with their innocent, long-lashed eyelids slid back, the ones wrapped in a torn, gunpowder-stained flag? Where is *her* father now, putting his hand through the bay window one night, years before I was born, thrusting it into the black, iced-over waters as his girls slept upstairs?

Now he's drawing me onto his knee again, pulling the starched shirtcuff to his elbow. Now I'm running my finger up and down that crooked scar, palm to wrist, the bones tight with a skin pink as the tissue that covers the chest of a bald baby bird. He could hold a match to it for seconds.

Years later, when he was folded into a wheelchair, when he couldn't even light a cigarette—his wife would put one in his mouth each evening at 5:30—when his albums of stamps were locked behind cabinets of glass, waiting to be sold, when he couldn't speak so much as a word, the hand was the last to go. Lifting a nurse's skirt, or simply clenching and loosening by itself. But in the photograph, he's still a young man. He squats with his family on a cluster of sea-worn stones. His face, his whole bony frame, does not come alive, no matter how hard I stare, but floats and washes like driftwood in the black-and-white tides of 1949.

7:00 a.m. and the sun spilling its copper glow
across the fields. I stand with stones in my hand,
I look down and count the sheep
huddled in their shawls, carefully nosing the grass.
They turn each blade, I think,
searching for something
and follow a slight scent of clover to the brook.

I'm too far away to hear their bleating, although
I'm sure it's low, deep as the throb of well-oiled gears,
and human too—

even the soaked air
holds a faint cloud of exhaust above them.
My friend says that each season
they always lose a few: heartworm, pneumonia,
or those that just stop breathing.

Now the sheep are safe, floating lilies
on this green lake. And the steam

drifting in tatters, and the dew
soaked into the canvas of my tennis shoes.

And the light coming down hard, all over me.

I watched a lamb being born once.
He trembled before me, half-swallowed,

he paused, as if hesitating.
Sealed mouth, sealed eyes,
then pulled out into the morning light,
his whole numb body
folded and coated in those blinding juices.

For some reason, he just couldn't open.
I wanted to take him into my arms, there in the haydust
and black light of the barn, I wanted
to feel him at the joints, still hot from the machinery

of birth. As I stand here now, watching the sheep
drift below, I think of his broken grace,
how he shuddered once and opened to the great passage of air.

In my old sheepdream, I wander for days,
bending back the tall grass as I go.

I come to a river at last, and kneel
amongst the drinking sheep to let the water
run over my wristbone.

I sit up quietly into my body,
alone in the other dark, my hand cramped and curled into my gut,
aching. And somewhere back in the ammonia night
my mother's father floats. Somewhere back

behind his eyes, sheep after galloping sheep
follows a deadly scent down to the bank:
how slowly the moon draws its waters.

I'd like to wade back into those glassy embalming fluids, loosen the hook
from his neck, and lift his preserved body onto any dry land.
I'd like to lead him down by his one bad hand

to the bank of some sheepfold river,
where one horse turns the trampled weeds gently with its nose,
and the stars burn overhead like steel.

DEPRESSION GLASS: A LETTER

Dear trace of carbon,

Dear fingerprint, left behind in this gloss,
hat to one side; wanting,
                         for so many years to reach
into this photograph
                         and touch your tweed,
to break the glass.

Dear listener, Dear slick, dirty fossil—

                              tonight we *are* the dead.

Staring out through this buckled glass,
                         through the eyes of that dead soldier

nobody had thought to close until now,
the one who lay gently in tall grass, in that photograph from the war,
the one I found as a boy,
                         tucked into one of your stamp albums,

our eyes half-closed, swollen, lifeless, cracked.
You do an admirable impression of a river

the way you run in and out of my life,
                         the way we go about our dying, slowly—

                         it's a kind of drink.

I kneeled in the grass by the homeless river just now,
and asked for a sip:

                         Sam, you coughed into my hands
If the heart is a blood sandwich,
                         what can we do
but sit down and eat?

Tonight, I'm eating alone.
I'm standing here,

alive in this other photograph, the one I love, off to myself.

We are sharing a body before the war,
beside your hated in-laws, in the ranks of a stunned choir—

it must be us, smiling your smile—affectionate, but miles away—here,
in an orchard,
                    before the hidden still—it must be us,
dripping through the copper tubes, breathing these fumes,
                         about to cough, our bubbling spirits
coming to life in those buckled, tin vats.

We are drifting and rising
                    like moonshine smoke,

Dear smudged benediction:
somewhere, deep within these veins,
                    our sourmash burns without a flame,
lifting its thin smile,

cold as the oil that burns these waters
for good tonight,
                    on this side of the James.

Your cough wants to say
the river has slashed its narrow wrists;
                              here we go again.
But instead of water, sheets of glass

are falling out of the sky, we're falling

through layer after layer of bloodstained glass,

because you are dreaming me:
                              and just as we hit the ground,

just as I realize that our hands
                              have a little death of their own,

a headlight touches my brow, and I'm awake,

in a different orchard, here, by the river, a green shoot
splitting my scarred bark,
                              a shard of glass clenched in your bony fist.

Nothing up above but sky,
                              flashed by sheets of heat lightning.
Now it darkens to the cracked tint
of Depression glass.

                              Nothing but slag angels,
drifting above the dockyards,
                              nothing on the other bank
but a fire, breathing up
                              from its steel drum when you snap your fingers:
it must be me, a young mare
that waters here each night, Dear tramp, burning—

it must be us, the river
                              drinking itself dry in my wet hands,
Dear species of dust,
                              Dear us, a fine ash I breathe—

Take my hand kid,
                              Step out with a bow.

SEIZURE *(Later)*

Outside my window,
I can hear cows,
bellowing in a field of steam,

their breaths threading together
slowly, under streetlamps,
rising over the tulips

like lead balloons:
the garbage trucks
clang together

like barges,
and sound across the black waters
of this city:

somewhere back in the depths
my father's dark business suit
tightens around him like skin,

across the black waters
of this skinless rain:
my temple nailed to the pillow:

some part of us
washed up by the flashflood
on a neighbor's pool table:

lays its drowned cow
across that green altar
until—

LATE SUMMER FEVER

for Graves Truesdale

The breath of the pregnant mare was coming in gasps.
She stamped her hindlegs twice when I walked into the barn.

I remember crossing four of Hervie's fields that day
to watch the colt being born;

past the sheep that ran in circles all day long,
cowbirds gathered in the ash tree by the barn,

small as flies from where I stood,
coils of electrical fencing, the smell

of ammonia & fire: how she bucked when I got too close, shied wildly,
& then her thigh muscles rippled as they shivered open & forgot me,

a coarse, golden static suddenly blazing the haydust.

—————————————

                      Once, as a boy, they put me in a bathtub of ice
to break my fever.

The bird with a tail of so many bright colors, that whispered its heat
    into my ear,
was my only friend. Not those tall shapes,

moving so far above me, but a blue ripple,
I was born with a caul on my head

the shadows of birds passing across the surface of my stomach.

—————————————

& then it appeared, as though drifting: a tiny, half-formed, blue face,
recently undrowned from its birthwaters, almost human.

I felt so small as a ripple once the ice had melted,

39

the ice that gave its form to my heat . . .

& the mare shifted, & pushed, a black muscle rippling
as her colt eased down through several human arms,

down there where my long, black hair floated
like the silk of a horse's drowned mane.

Snuffed tongue of my fever still licking the inside of my ear,
lay there like driftwood in the straw for the mare to lick,

worn smooth by a current.
And it stood for a moment in the August light,

on thin legs that buckled to one side, then folded at the knees
as the mare began to lick its head.

Licking its last heat from my forehead—no,

all we could think to do was cut & tie the cord anyway,
that was my mother's hand.

Struggled, turned blue, lifted a crinkled, pink ear, & its chest
swelled just once, then fell,

what I remember is my hearing, suddenly blotted open
as they pulled me up into the screaming of cicadas,

under some blind weight, an invisible blue palm pressing down,
the oaks, lashing like breakers to a sudden calm,

& my temples were born again, as the grass
rushed away in a single ripple from the barn.

& the other horses shifted & stamped in their stalls,
the ash tree tossed open in the wind & began to breathe.

& the air filled with that small death,
the way the smell of rain fills a forest before it breaks.

—————————————————

Through the cracked barn-door you could hear it,
breath for breath across the yard—& then the colt

pulling itself out, still folded, blind, root & glazed vein,
slab of its side half-swallowed, I gasp,
                                  as if drawn from water.

All they could think to do was leave me there,
lit by chaff on the floor.
                         In the dream that keeps coming back
in the shape of a barn, I'm breathed out over water,

my heart dancing like a small flame on the surface.
I'm lifted

& set back down, into a body, in a barn.
& then the colt coming out crippled,

limb for bent limb, I try to lift it; I'm folded,
then opening, then rising up slowly

like haydust, like nothing at all into the stillness,
the heavy light of late summer.

PERIOD

I.

The waters shift and gather, tadpole and lily,
a fistful of spawn: the slow blur of night
coming on like a bruise. I am out here,
floating in a rowboat, unanchored, a faint glow, mist
of a body, the katydids and the crickets
stitching a small scar through the night.

I lean over the gunwhale, and a face pops to the surface,
suspended in the frogwaters. Then another, and another,
blunt nostrils puffing in and out, a tiny half-moon
beaded in each eye. I lean over, and fists of green lard
punch up one by one, bloated and angry—hoosh, plop—
then slapdashing away across the skipped surface,

scattering away into the juniper berry night.
The mutilated, sperm-dark waters shift, and gather a response,
wriggling with tadpoles when I dip my hand to the wrist.
And I can feel the old ache of blood
with each rise and fall of my gut,
seeping down runnels and creekbeds of my body.

I remember the wild geese calls falling out of the darkness.
I remember the catalpa leaves, big enough to cover a boy's face,
the morning light so heavy it almost dissolved the window-panes,
as it fell into my room.
            The day I found her underpants
in the sink, I didn't know what they were, stained and floating there
like a jellyfish. I could have lifted them, as a boy lifts a lilypad,
weighted by its single root, and glimpses the tail of a brim
flashing back down the darkness.

I am a soaked lily, folded around a breath of fire.

I am going to close my eyes and drift back blind.

Flutter. Pulse of a wing. A lost flap
through the branches. In the molt and roost of the swallows,
in the lapping water, I can feel the movement of blood.
Even now the sunlight sleeps in the leaves,
stirring the small hearts of tadpole, and brim—

                      even now I still sometimes sleep

as if I'd not been born.

2.

When my mother was a girl, German POWs worked the streets of Richmond. It wasn't uncommon in those days to wake up to the clink of a chain, to a sledgehammer striking cobblestone and its echo, like a horse's shod hoof, the voices singing out together into the early morning air. *The night he put his hand through the bay window, she was just a girl.*

Down the wooden hall, the lacquered floor worn smooth as a pew by generations of bare feet, past the dining room, where a battered silver bowl sat on the sideboard, filled with dried rose petals and dead bees. *His girls were sleeping upstairs the night he put his hand through the glass.*

Down the front hall, past the mahogany-and-glass cabinet where he kept his stamp albums, the tall bony man in plain pants and a cardigan, each of his etched faces sealed in mylar and pressed down, past the long freezer from the thirties, with each of its legs of lamb frozen solid, its fanbelts mumbling, *they woke to a tinkling sound of breaking glass and a moan, the night he put his hand through that black ice.*

Down the slanted cellar steps, two bronze panels of sunlight, coming through the painted, starling-cracked window panes like a magician's blades. I was twelve when I found his shirt in a cardboard box that afternoon, torn and spattered like a surgeon's smock, wrapped around a luger, beside a gunpowder-stained flag, neatly folded around three bullet holes: *the night she watched her mother tighten his shirt around that bony wrist . . .*

3.
My mother told me tonight on the phone that when her students bleed on
the playground, she's not allowed to bandage the cut without putting on
latex gloves. She watches them as they grow tired, the sun sinking behind a
housing project, heavy and pregnant and smog-swollen red.

Each spring one or two of her students always disappears without a word.
The worst part, she told me, when their faces begin to fade, when only a
name is left, Leander, and Joshua, and Kim: their names drift across the
pages of her book like the shadows of passing birds.

But it's nightfall now, and my mother sleeps, and the children are at play.
They are calling out, they are laughing, they have vanished now into the tall
grasses of her sleep. Their faces rise like rain-beaten stones, and disappear
one by one . . . and her father's drained face among them,

the blood sleeping in each small body, the same small measure beating
fainter and fainter through her darkness until she wakes alone . . .

4.
Sunlight through a weed: the fallen rain
spreading back into black branches now.
With all my breathing, out of me, the dead grow
into these ribs: this hand: this jawbone's line
is their way. Their thin voices sing through our skin
in sleep, even that one whose voice was low,
and fill our lungs—no, tonight they are snow,
lightly tapping the frozen window pane.

Your father, for one, who'd toss me into the air
—easily as he lifted the glass, caught on his start—
then let go, and for a long second, I'd soar.
It's been twenty years since that last night.
Did it open its fist into the dogwood's rainy blur
just to let me fall? Or clench that tired heart.

RECIPE FOR THE FIRE

for Graves Truesdale, 1963-1994

All day long I've been touching
these emblems of hunger—
hinges, rusted shut,
stewing on the stove in your favorite pot: the television,
smearing its dropsied face all over this room;
the cat, sullen, padding by.
I touch the bloated cluster of ticks
rooted to the inside of its left haunch. If *you* were alive,
maybe you'd follow her outside too, as I do now,
and crack a matchflame on your thumbnail and hold it
to each tick until it sizzles and pops,
and feel those fattened birds somewhere up above,
cooing the air with their belly-rumble,
and taste this hunger
the dead don't feel.
     Snow, piled up against
the porch-door, the heating grill.
The car engine will not turn over. I've spent all day
cleaning out your ice-box, and found there,
just now, under the ziplocked marjoram
and dill, between a solo Hungry-Man
and a crusted bottle, 2 fingers full,
this frozen dove—wings splayed, eyes
flashing like a cat's pupil
in the dark.

One heap of uncured hay,
genuine barnburner, pitched onto the snow.
Three birch-limbs, leftovers from last season:
denatured, gasoline-doused, flayed, crossed.
One pillowcase your head imprinted.
One telephone, the receiver
your lips touched
maybe fifty times. Lace curtains

that recognize me
and shiver, a single match
that burns my thumb:

This is *your* fire.

For later, you said, tossing the bird into the freezer.
Later: snapped neck, broken wing; in the branches, a bag of fat.
I remember the cat, scratching at the door
almost politely, a message for you, still alive in her jaws.
Now, months past, ankle-deep in snow,

the snow burying even my footprints,
I can feel your needles under my wing.
And then the cat must have dropped her prize, because suddenly,
the bird was beating its one good wing
in the corner, beside the capsized dish of milk;

and as you lifted it, wasn't that *us,*
stiffening and dying, that look of astonishment in your hands?

Mourning doves, perched on the phone-lines,
so late in December—it's no dream, these

voices that have grown into fattened bodies,
these lumps of dough,

really, blood-swollen, baked out in the cold.
It's no delusion:

in that pulse, steady and purring,
I hear your heart, jump-started again,

and you hate me for the dove-breast
I ate in Paris, glazed

in apricot preserve and stuffed with wild rice.
When I think of your death,

I see sperm, smeared and frozen
on a window pane; from that beady-eyed,

mewling little heaven, I see you hating me
for the cigarette cherry my life has burned to

as my lungs pinch in the cold.

One newspaper, crumpled
around happy words, kerosene-soaked,
deep with trouble and ink,
touched into flame:

this was your brain.

One pinch of pure
snow, pure enough to kick a mule's chest
still: one hunk of fat, snagged
in the ribcage, one broken wing:

this was your stopped heart.

The parlor of a funeral home.
A backyard. Just this morning, right now—
one rosary, collapsing unstrung
into the flames:

these were your teeth.

One suit, crumpled and stuffed
with uncured hay, sliding down the chute—this
was your ash, rising now from the fire,
a sprinkle of eyelash, a handful of cheek and hair:

snow, fall now, evacuate the industrial sky

of your black, incinerated hair, and let me go.
Mingle, and melt here now above the flames:
one dove, wrapped in phone-cord,
tossed into the fire: this,

your gift to me.

THE BLOOD ORANGE

I thought if I dug
deep enough I'd find it
your face turning towards me
out of the frozen dirt

myself
walking downstairs just now
—the ruptured insides of your elbow
still nailed into my ribcage

and woke to a window
left open a plate of orange sections
by the telephone
a dish of frozen milk

The blood orange is human
in 3 ways

Its meat is abundant
with burst burgundy veins
Its sweetness resembles
a kind of bleeding

like you
It smiles when cut

Human—
the tall body laid out
beneath its sheet
Skin steeped in bleach
a little blue
your hooked nose protrudes

as if you could smell
my breathing

filling the room
with the scent of an orange
the moment its skin
was broken:

You
not coming towards me now
across the backyard
populated with ice
You lift your punctured arms
(Come towards me now)
You step behind a dormant poplar
signaling yes

it *was* delicious to breathe after all
especially those last sweet times
Come here
I lift

this fleshy peck of ice
this fistful
of crushed glass
to my lips

It freezes my tongue

Then your juices
burning into both sides of my cheek
On this side
You are not alive:

the window gaping half-open
the receiver resting
bluntly on its cradle
feeling my face turn away

the branches living with ice
splinters of frozen milk
I am here now but
did you have to kill us

did you have to kill us
every day

NEW RIVER BLUES

Saying to the river   STOP
Saying stop to the miserable little riffles as they flash past—

a hundred years ago this morning
I dreamt your body was a box of ash [it is]
and woke up, saying: Come back.
Back to that place where
You went to sleep in the backseat of a Pacer,
"in an accident, in a car."
Stopped breathing, turned blue,
just more human traffic
crossing the Golden Gate Bridge.
Afraid of that place in me
where everything that ticks has stopped,
afraid of this exhumed and crumbling air
you became.

Looking down at the broken waves, I hum—

a hundred years ago this morning I passed the traffic cop
nodding off on the corner on his beat: crossed
a recently shaven hill where drowsy cows,
their left ears tagged,
still rock from side to side
swishing flies to sleep on their hides—

Looking up through the railroad ties
that stitch the gaping blue sky, I fall asleep a bit
and hum, and hum—

I followed these snuffed fuses of milkweed young
from stalk to stalk
down a bank where the grass runs in place
to where they fell just now like cotton wadding
into this pool.

Looking down, I dream a washer for each cold eye.
Looking up, I dream the Polestar
[stopped breathing. turned blue.] and hum
same old car that brought you there
gonna carry you home again [STOP—]

All my bells
have put out their tongues for you.
Lifting my arms, I make a perfect, dirty space
for the wind to fill:
looking down through my feet,
looking down into the river's hush and hurry,

I listen to the touched sun fall:
["It was no accident   I couldn't   STOP
spinning in that furious, blue sinkhole of years
into this living rage still punctured into my arm"]

Graves, it's no accident—

you are turning blue again:
["I feel so clean"]
                    in this place,
where the light flashes and flashes a single ripple
repeatedly into the torn, reflected sky
like a stuck second hand that ticks, and ticks
the same cold space a thousand times: into this place
where the river wrinkles like tinfoil,
looking down, I travel swiftly,
pierced into this clear, broken skin with its dozen suns,
looking down, I travel swiftly north
but do not move.
Feeling the leaves turn in place
on the filthy, immaculate shore.
Feeling the dull clapper of my tongue move:

I was wrong.
Keep us dirty for a hundred years,
let my skin burn the icy water along
as I step to my knees
you are going out again
you are turning blue behind smoked glass
you are whispering   STOP
to your incinerated breath   come back

BLACK PONY ON A BANK OF THE JAMES

Simple blood & mass, simple machinery—
acres downriver from the paper mills,

head curled into its own long shadow, decorticated
& grazing . . .

stopped by the river long enough to say your name:
Knucklebone, empty, porcelain head.

Stopped breathing long enough dead child to say your name:
when your faces are washed from me in a grassly painful rain,

mouthful of white powder & *felt you,*
pulled from me into its black, cideling eyes

for their small, reflected sunset blood to thin,

running at the corner with tears of rheum, & dew,
that the light lay down its tiny eggs into our eyes,

& feed you, with the other palm pressed
to the pony's gently swelling side, for a long time

I listened to your empty grazing in the river's echo, & hish . . .

Once, as kids, in an orchard, before dawn,
you stroked the flashlight beam across a pony's dwarfed,

powerful back: his side was rising gently, falling, then rose,
like a giant wineskin stretching its seams through that circle of three,

rolling a waterdrop down his hide,
& I stepped back into you, a tiny, human spark from your hand

suddenly going out in its eye, & we both inhaled,
but the pony didn't wake.

Of human beastliness, I sleep in my feet,
a handful of sugar: a muzzle-kiss: a smoking thumb

lifting its luscious neck now when I approach,
such gentle breeding that I walk in my walking sleep,

a black gelding with its left ear torn & healed.
I step forward, I stop myself, a hand on its swelling flank.

I too am a starveling, all five stomachs half-full.

I too am slipping away with a withers, a hum,
with each heft & sink,

grooving its ruin into my palm: Contagion, empty me

to a riffling breeze, a tail that twitches, & lifts,
to each horse-apple as it strikes, in darkness, the ground,

& smolder me awake.

& when the stallion within steps forth to breath, I sing:
each of us threaded together through our tearducts,

Why do you tear me, child, with the memory of *your* breathing?
With that morning when the breath passed from horse to horse,

& they suddenly woke with a scream,
a dozen starlings exiting a chimney

to a sudden, earful hush, & broke, *that I am dead,*
& stretch my darkling seams?

AUBADE IN BLUE

for Richard Spottswood Clay Witt, 1968—

Jesus O jesus. Bloodflick and release,
a changed lid spun anew, loving the eye: the nerves,

the blue nerves taking root
like a blue fever at the base of the spine.
I'm thinking of the glass barrel of a syringe,
the one you used as a cigarette holder. I'm thinking
of last spring—*Come on, Sam,*
how your back hunched a little
as I bent the needle down under my thumb,
and my fingers slipped, and the thin steel snaps

all over again, your thorn sliding snugly under my skin.
And believe it, what we share,
as brothers, we share alone:
splinter of disease, a clear path in the veins—
its blue drift back up the bloodstream
to where it snags home like a hook in the heart.

The window swallows its three stars.
Drugged, swollen, somewhere below
the line of mountains, the moon
hangs, bloated as a drowned child.
Uprisen, pierced by the stars,
what you see is what we'll always see:
soft nest of the Shenandoah, the hills
shoring up into its blue froth and moaning
like lazy whales. You see the rivers,
heavy, flashing to steel, Otter Creek
tightening like piano wire, cutting the land:
the Bullpasture, the Occoquan, steel.

It burns like a sulfur prayer, burns so badly some mornings, I hold a lit
   match to the inside of my arm, and slowly count to three.
Here's my grandfather's straight-razor that kissed my skin, when I ran
   out of veins.
A little face bubbles and smiles in its spoon.
Here's my forearm, white as the underwing of a gypsy moth, and here,
   the red-and-purple braille I can no longer read.
Then a few stars came out to heal.
Through the buckled window I saw a valley pierced with lights. Called
   it the valley of the shadow of life.
Night sky of tiny blue, my own blue little crescent-moon of glass.
Blue mountains, blue little deathribs, wrinkling off to my tinfoil ocean,
   which sparked and tossed.
Shot a little battlehymn into my arms—O glory, glory—it sank through
   my laced skin.
Then all the world was sleeping.
Dropped the spoon and it clattered, a thousand-and-one spears.
Then slowly, slowly from within, I could feel it slowly rise, in the sweet
   scent of horsehair burning clean.
Pulled at my arm and it came out singing like a thin child.

SUNFLOWER-BROTHER

I. Poppyship

Nights like these he visits:
                         fistful of needles, jar of fireflies
dying like an ancient, walled city on the sill.
I can't see it,
              this black fire

softly folded home, this window pane that drips
as he drifts from room to room.

Here in the kitchen, the pendulum swings off-time.

Here, everything and nothing swings off-time.
I can't see him,
               I can't see him, he's alive: a sunflower, unfolding
out of these spiny needles drawn with dew, it bursts into flame,

the blazing pupil of a God, then pinpoints to an eye, just a child's, really,
              there, a Japanese paper flower that blooms

into this little junkyard of lights
                     in the window's black waters.
I feel him like broken glass,
               swimming in my veins,
nights like these—

His arm won't bleed, empty blue sleeve.
His porcelain head will not break.

O long-lashed, innocent eyelids slid back,
that's *his* breathing,
               all around me. Then it echoes to a tick.
Little ocean of breath,
              I bury you in my clenched fist,

I put you to my ear; doubled over, I listen.

It ticks again: alive, alive.
I'm blowing my fist into a mass of faintly glowing glass,

a bottle, and just when it hardens,
                    just when I call it brother,
                                    we are sinking
into its immense belly,
                    we are tiny now, a ship
of skin-and-bone, carrying its immensely expensive cargo
of blood and nerve,
double-helixing down into this black, down,

into little nothing-waves as we breathe.

2. The Sunflower

Shadow of an arm, blueprint of veins
etched into the night sky; I limp through the hanging garden,
my left leg dead as a pendulum,
                    an axe that won't swing.

The valley of your elbow slides into the Milky Way.
Like bruised stars, like caterpillar eggs
shining on a bed of black leaves, your trackmarks
pulse into their own aurora borealis:

one half of your skin lies on the horizon's side,
its purple veins shaken down, glowing like a marbled seam.

One half of your breath fills the ash-tree's empty suits.

If the breeze carries a scent of burning tar and hay,
if the ash tree lifts its cancerous robes

to reveal a knotted gut of piano wire and gear,
the shadow of its side slapped with grease,
I know it's you.
                    Black luminous dew,

beloved of garden spiders and hummingbirds,
black venom, the outer leaves shredded

like torn rags—ah, Sunflower-brother,
faceless young god of the weedpatch,

I limp to your sulfur-glow,

seedless pregnancy, explode!

3. <u>Within</u>

You will be discarded like the days that anticipate winter;
rooted like the dead, whose thought touching fingers
limp toward the sun. Lift your toothless head.
The Son of the flower has risen, not quite a man;

rooted like the dead, whose thought touching fingers
explore the sulfur-darkened sockets of fallen seeds.
The Son of the flower has risen, not quite a man:
I stare into its slumbering golden face,

explore the sulfur-darkened sockets of fallen seeds.
Where a black seed should rest, where ants pull a bee's wing,
I stare into your slumbering golden face
and read the words tattooed into that Bible of yellow skin.

Where a black seed should rest, where ants pull a bee's wing,
the eye limps deeper like an eye—it doesn't pause
to read the words tattooed into these Bibles of yellow skin:

our sins, our aluminum sins. It's candlelit,

the eye limps deeper like an eye. Don't pause
by the rooms, the empty chairs, by the stained windows that sing
our sins, our aluminum sins; it's candlelit
within. And like one lost body, we wander

by the rooms, the empty chairs, by the stained windows, we sing:
remember me, and wake into this tiny burning field,
within; you are just one lost body wandering
through my meadow lit by another sunflower's torch.

So we remember, and wake into a vastly burning field,
and like a drunk shepherd, call the flock back home,
through a meadow lit by another sunflower's torch—
our beloved, our dirty little black-faced sheep. They're coming, too.

Like a drunk shepherd, have I really called the flock back home?—
sugarfluffs, soft eggs the moon has lain:
my beloved, my dirty little black-faced sheep:
emptiness yawns at a stone's throw in the grass.

Sugarfluff, soft egg the moon has lain,
cricket legs are building a matchstick gallows in the cracks,
at a stone's throw, where emptiness yawns in the grass:
this little sheep sinned at market.

Cricket legs are building a matchstick gallows in the cracks,
we cannot see their tiny threads of song—
this little sheep sinned at home—
which pierce between the ribs of our fading, woolen side.

I cannot see their tiny threads of song
from which I hang, and as each dirty snout lovingly strokes the wound
pierced between the ribs of our fading, woolen sides,
they fall, these yellow thoughts of within,

and lovingly stroke our dirty snouts, our wound,
and like the discarded days that anticipate winter,
we rise on a thread, one yellow thought of within.
Sunflower-brother, lift your toothless head:

we are limping at last toward the sun.

Three

CONFESSION

Call it a meadow of combustible air,
fifty feet from the parking lot. Love,
if you could read my palm right now, you'd feel it:
an oilcan fire, a tramp, some burning tires.
You'd feel the radiant half-life of our country,
at rest under my finger, a continent,
really, collapsing as my hands part

and it slips between the cracks,
something I can't touch, something to make my fingers
cramp up and hate themselves,
when I reach out to you. The truth is,

I love this world.
Sometimes part of me even loves
what we've done to it: a child burying lead soldiers
after the war's over, for instance,
not fifteen feet away in this meadow, is a good thing.
I wonder if he sees me. I wonder
if that crumpled piece of tinfoil,
spitting up jagged little eclairs of light
between us, wakes his eyes

as they woke me just now, oil on my hands.
Call it what you will: a leaf, a stone,
a nameless lake of space we drift upon.
The truth: it's a lie—it doesn't move without you.
The truth: we are alone.

If you could read my palm,
you'd know I'm something like a virgin right now,
a field sown with gunpowder, something like the deer's skull
my brother immersed in motor oil, years ago,
in a cast iron tulip, a kind of perfect little ecosystem
in suspension. I can feel it now, rooted in the back of *my* neck,

as the copper light anoints each cheek.

There's a name for it,
when I reach out to you and find myself alone,
not helplessness or self-hatred, exactly.
If we could sleep together in that inner garden of breath,
it would not be a human zoo; rather, a place. I might have believed
it isn't possible to drown in an abandoned meadow, fifteen feet
from my country, a lost child I could speak to.

SEVENTEEN YEAR SLEEP

I didn't want to bury myself alive
    in this private little desert.

Feeling the cicadas chew into the nape of the air,
    into its green brainstem, into the wasted nerveshadows
of their song . . . I didn't want to lie here
        for seventeen years,

belly-up in a field,
my perfectly dried body left behind at dusk
still clinging to a leaf
in its hollow, translucent shell,
hunched around this thirsty shadow
as my breathing fell
and the drum-like sound chambers in my stomach
began to rattle and click.
Feeling the burdock take root
in my stomach, and the sand
burn in my sticky throat:
wheezing a little, trying my empty prayers,
alone at first,
this breathing *was* human.
Then joined by my cousins, all at once,
as they shredded the air en masse up above
with this shrill, wasted tongue,
sipping the dusklight until it thinned in my ear,
and filled with a sudden roar,
all ten thousand of them
shredding the air to confetti
with their razory wings:

    Black Locust, Black Chestnut, from tree to tree,
        let your sweet leaves stir.

Let them dream of a shudder, or two,

69

as I burrow through the dewbeaded,
blue-and-purple throat of this morning glory
        to wholly disappear,

a tuft of the sun in my mouth.
Let it dream that the sky
was an endless pane of darkening glass, and I,
a flushed bumblebee,
skittering its flaky, black fingerprint of wings against me,
against my cheek's glass shelf of sky:
Sam, those were beads of sipping dew
that were your eyes—there,
there, now. Your trembling lips
are sewn shut and fluttering still,
along with the lips of your gaping, empty eye:
we are drawing through your dry
tear-duct this horse-tail hair
of a song: now,
now that you've swallowed your tongue,
we're crawling out of your crumbled ear,

        like us, like us, out of that burrow-hole,
                the dry shadow

of a small, coiling wing, *let him be lifted,*
        through which you used to hear.
And now that the sky
        is leaning down

to lift you,
in swarming scales of us,
from the sockets
of your blinded eye,
you're picked clean,
raised into these green pockets,

to chew ourselves upward
through the sweet thirst
of this green, sleeping gut.
It's only us:
only the tree grown hysterical tonight,
in ribbons of shredded song:
us: leaf on leaf,
as we enter this caterwaul of green smoke
and chew it to a buzzing lace
before suddenly coiling back down
through the desiccated navel
of dusk
to a lingering drone—

then silence.

LAND OF MILK AND HONEY

after Magritte

I.
Thus I stood on the bank of a lake,
before the house a dead man built.

I could not enter because there's no door.
My father is a boy, cupping our palms:

& I am a boy too. He looks down: night.
I look up into the sky: daylight.

Together we cut a tiny figure.
Perfect baby blue a stone could crack.

Perfect sky. A few clouds surrender
like eroded flags because the war's on.

You didn't even let me say goodbye to her,
a breeze the color of sorrow

has crept into those branched lungs:
sugar-maple, fire-oak, elm . . .

Burns up above us
in the tumbrels of a single Harvest Fly;

spreads through the leaves, a rumor
of fire: *your mother's dead,* & now,

the others are screaming along
like the sex of trees, like sex

fallen darkly away from my body.
Stops on a dime, a chromosome

of silence: a little space: *Ssshhhh* . . .

There.　　　There, now,

for daylight has replaced the air,
& the clouds are in such a hurry,

suddenly tumbling overhead
like sea-blooms,

now they drift around my dipped wrist
& in *her* face, drown the half-sky above the silt.

2.
So much is seeing a part of light
that we are in the sky now
& already the house is buried in snow
Come on in the house, Sugar.
But there's no door　*Ssshhhh . . .*
It's no use standing out there, barefoot in the snow & yes
Somebody is writing this down
in a book full of clouds
Come on, upstairs. She's waiting for you.
has stained her tiny quill with our blood
Spread thinly through the vapors
of a cloudy hip but Mama
the piano keys darken when I play them
Leave the piano be & in the hallway
by the stopped grandfather clock it's dark
Come on out there from behind the curtains.
Even years later now they stir & breathe like skin:
Ruptured riverbeds　　　drowned veins down below
I didn't mean to scrawl my pain across the sky
A few shredded nerves drift off
like picked cotton
Can't feel my arms　　　my fingertips
Stained　　　washed through

This morning they clipped mama's spine
Light the wick and see but it hurts too much to look *I'm in here*
A Virgin Mother candle, a handful of honeyflame
No: it's a bowl of warm milk I've brought you
scorched at the edges *Come closer*
But mama, what's wrong?
Cancer's a funny thing, a little like you & me.
But the bed's empty : I'm in here
Lift the glass bowl to your lips, drink the honey in the milk,
taste it & see,
but mama it hurts *& look at me*
where our lip-marks touched,
& fossilized together, there on the glass rim,
a violet moth now flickers its papery wings into flame.
Careful now—by the wing, that's right, lift it
but mama, it hurts *now let it go*
& already I'm falling into snow
into droplets of frozen blood
through sheets of freezing air
as I kiss her vapory forehead through
to the pillowcase: already the house is buried
it hurts to touch & you wake up alone
Standing barefoot in the snow

FIREFLIES

for Mary Draper Witt, May 29, 1909 - July 23, 1940

Whatever is called now,
phosphorescence smeared between my finger & thumb;
whatever dust I breathe, & glow, window
without a face, sick & invisible, your skin
mapped out by the doctors
like a new world,
like *my* skin, in the glass, as I pass through it
into the mating bark of an owl,
sliding off your cancerous wrist
& into my throat,
whatever I mean to you:
I have been given a foretaste of yesterday: the tumor
coiled like an electric eel in your spine,
your spine,
hanging just now from the coat-tree as I made my way out back; the air,
why do you feel it; sparks of electricity,
conducted through the air that joins us
& keeps us apart,
why do you feel it, & kill me again. Not your corpse
laid out on the sideboard
as I walked outside with a lid-punctured jar, not thirty seconds ago,
but now——the mouth that is not a mouth
for I could not speak
opening, fireflies
swarming from it, these
agitated hosannas clustering to my heat
as I do my slow dance, my breathlessness, my quiescence,
these flies to a ruptured deer.
A quiet soughing in the leaves——not your voice
singing just now,
nor mine,
moving like a blue deer through the doorframe,
then the weeds,
rinsed alive in your sparking lymph,

my dewclaws rubbed tender, my false hoof—
but a woman, letting her long hair down at last
when I drop your silver hairpin.
Sugar-trace in my veins, painful sugar
on the tongue; leaves that hiss as they rush,
meaning you: a kind of mother, I guess: a kind of living braille
that pulses through me in the backyard: eyes
carried in the fingertips:
a green tear, smeared like anti-freeze on my cheek
when a firefly lights there, & I kill it.
Can't you see I had to tear myself back down
& blow apart like dandelion-fluff that glows
as the air moves, a celebration
of scars, unknitting themselves into diaspora,
into a new skin for us,
in this shower of sulfurous life.
I am entering your willow infested with light;
I am broadcasting exactly what—pleasure? fear?
That sex-cry through the window? You? The one
seeing this sex torn now from the air,
now, flickering off again, & on again, now, & now,
this girl with her bloodletting jar?
I wanted to be, I wanted to be
Put to sleep by your touch: a finger for each heavy eyelid
more than just meat: dewdrops soldered to the leaves
for half a century, or more.
How can they rise?

JERUSALEM

Once again I have wakened
just to enter the animal of this body.
Even in the prison of this body, I can sing with my fingers
in a barely whispered scream again,

just by pulling apart this morning glory bloom
to find you wriggling inside of it,
pollen-drunk, fumbling, alive, a bumblebee this time:
even in the prison of your missing body

that comes at me from everywhere at once,
like an underwater scream,
I am capable of silence: I put a petal in my mouth,
from which your finger has been amputated,

& suckle until I'm filled
with a bitter violent wriggling from inside of which,
my fingers open this tuft of yellow pain.
Open you up into this nest of air, & from here,

from the place in my palm
that once cupped your hip, an invisible zero
traced here in yellow chalklines of trembling,
you take flight now, pulled into its buzzing body

that leaves behind a residue of yellow salt:
this body, that suffers the world brightly: this breath,
snatched in a gasp from my lungs, this spiderweb
catching you in its embrace . . .

The kissed web trembles, animal-snag, & I,
standing here dumbly am an entirely alternate
shudder system, embracing three flowers
in a gaze of moving air.

The moving air mimes your spine in the linens,

suddenly it blooms on the clothesline like a sail,
then empties with a snap to the hero's deflated smock,
this laughing breeze that snaps

into a clutter of clothespins, then stillness,
then slaps its way through catalpa leaves
until I can feel each dewdrop fall
from the tips of those heartshaped skins,

each flayed dewdrop of honeysuckle & lilac
lined with your face,
rinsed through the bitter taste of your eyes,
I spill out into the air

& rattling into a river
of busted windowshield glass,
it litters the flower touched weeds,
as the catalpa pods shake their dried seeds with a hiss.

The wall is where I take space.
I give tongue here in a silent weeping.
The wall is silence where I give.
I can hear my heart beating against it,

when I press my ear to the wall; my eyes,
glittering these touched weeds
with such pentecostal fire
that a bitter, jerusalem animal I am become:

the sapphire in my tongue is coated in poison:
your finger, still moving in my mouth was a place,
where we pulled each other apart,
& the body that's left behind, this space

I sing from is nothing, bright web,

nothing cleared from these stalks by a finger, a breeze, a you,
shuddering awake inside,
then sipped into nowhere through the emptied dew;

no, where the murdered air breathes *us*,
the web broke,

& you decayed into flight, & flew.

MORNING SONG

Once again I can feel each burning flea
rooted nerve-deep in life's wool,
and because I discover my hands early this morning,
I will lie here until death do us shave,

forgetting the stones, the grass,
the green horses of the weather, forgetting the birds
which strike the ground like dull fists;
clicking on and off with those scattered bits of machinery

that crackle like grasshoppers,
counting only the painful little dirges
that tapdance down my vertebrae with each step
as my sheep grow larger.

Each bleary eye is a sullen raindrop,
refusing to fall. I know I've felt those dirty clouds before,
the ones they wear on their grass-stained backs.
They're so close I know those dry, ancient little noses

are about to nuzzle my young cheeks.
Because I reach out to them with my accidental hands,
once again they will count off one by one
like ragged soldiers bleating for morphine—

because I'm pulling this knit skin
back over my head like a sweater, because
I'm counting my ribs and calling them sheep,
having closed up the flesh instead thereof,

once again they will lay down their ancient blood
into my shadow and rise singing glory,
forever clumsy, forever young, happy in their milk,
their lost element and glow, wobbling once again

on those newly split feet
through this burning meadow,
where there are no sharp blades or shears.
Because they are marching to my slaughter

like a battle hymn,
because I love myself too much,
I'm down to this broken flute, this spine,
counting sister, lover, firstborn,

my last bright sheep cursed with a brain.

BIBLE BURNING

There are three decapitated sunflowers
hanging out their empty lanterns
in the garden tonight,
and moths, reeling in a light
that is not ours;

but I am done with Ash Wednesday now.
Essence of soft air humming in the rain:
I remember the tin leaves
and there they are, laughing in the windchimes.
I remember the empty grate

and there sits my grocery bag of ash on the stoop,
ten pounds at least,
its paper bottom eaten apart by the rain.
I cannot shake this feeling:
like ash we are cleanest after burning.

I cannot rub this cross off
I drew on my forehead just now:
like ash we blow away.
Into this garden, a sudden hot rain lashes.
I am coming apart in its thrumming kiss.

I have plugged myself into this world
like the pear tree, fruit already welling
in its one great wound,
I remember the birds, fattened and purring
in those green pouches

and *here* I am,
flickering on and off; here, and here,
I wave my arms wildly like an infant
and clear a space for myself—
a thirsty garden I'm walking through.

Somewhere back behind the ear
I can hear a thousand tiny wings hum;
I can feel the ash sift down
from rib to rib, this bruised living
burning up,

stirring deep within this sack of skin.
I am eroded by each second, by each warm drop,
I must be down to a hundred pounds by now;
with a finger on my wrist, I listen
and walk—

Drop after hot drop
falls through these black leaves.
The tree measures my breathing tonight
like a fabulous waterclock:
I am alive: here,

and   here.
I am falling to the ground,
a warped, reflected sunflower, bursting
each raindrop's belly: there,
and there, a moth lost in the air,

the night become my shadow, blind,
hiding this scrap of light
beneath my inconceivably thin skin—as tonight,
how many times, the air bleeds,
and I am tied to it.

It's a kind of flesh I sift
through my fingers,
this painful bracelet of a pulse. I thrust
my hand into the bag and feel it under the wet crust,

the fine dust from under those wings.

I remember the fire and *here* it is,
a green breath that lifts me up
and drags me down,
this green life stitched into my loins,
O lovely disease:

my spine is a tuning fork,
fibrillating in Your pitch and thirst.
I am all skin, a beautiful shirt,
death-embroidered and throbbing,
a kiss consuming the air,

with a finger on my wrist,
with a green angel
swallowing my blood
in this cage of ribs,

I go, I go . . .

Consider that it might be
                    the last time this light slides
across my belly, its thirst
                    almost human;
its lingering generations Veronica and sift
                    through the window,
the scarf unwinds: yesterday, this morning, never, this
scattering of little nows.

                Do *you* feel it, listening there?—everything, nothing at all,
paused into the rivers of air;
                    burning so coldly, and with such hunger, I lie.
Certainly not alive—a woman's hair,
                    this falling over me—
certainly not a breath,
                though I'm wasting my breath,
exhaling a sexual dust
                  that sets my skin on fire.

It listens. Ecce, ecce—
                not a sound.
Do you feel it now,
                you there in the empty room—
                    brother? sister? friend?
Do you feel it flaying the air,
                a savage warmth
                    buried darkly under my skin,
do you feel this tension
                as the light tries to touch it?

We do not have souls, we have hands.
                    Unable to touch just now,
to reach out to nobody:
                the air, scarves of dust; hands,

I blame you.

In your greedy little city I lie,

                              the heart murdering itself.
I am falling now
                    into the world's harbor,
into the world's stomach,
                    a thousand years at a time.
                              Irradiated by this light,
I am a spark, a dog's tear
                    swallowing a puddle,
these fractures of starlight from within.
                              Hands, it's all so ancient and new.
Some day,
                    the world will chatter meaninglessly
up above us,
                    a payphone droning off the hook.
The light will harden,
                    and break into pieces,
                              and we shall reach out to them,
and fall into these intricate fissures.

                              A finger stirs and I discover it
—*stay there, light, stay there.*
                    Thou art fairer than the evening air—
                              cloaked in the beauty of a thousand suns.

No. Point blank,
                    it will continue to fall, a dropcloth
                              over the young ache in my shoulder blades,
over my frame,
                    a slender, crumpled chair:
                              thin as the skin over my chatoyant belly,
this dissolving to dust:
                    her shroud.
Lift it.   Let it fall.

I start by eating these words
the way that starling picks his wing-lice
on the window sill. I start here: a slight touch
of sunlight in your eyes; I'm following
these footprints as they spill from your mouth
down into the region of the stomach.

This tiny desert I bring to you,
drifting in my hands, signifies exile.
When I touch you, it's an oasis, miraged
on the air between us, a beautiful fingerprint
soaking the sheets with these skeletons of rain—
my tongue is listening in as it traces
a blue vein, and sets your arm free.

I call it freedom,
this tiny bird puffing its thin, bloody chest
in your wrist. I call it now,
an answer: do we belong to the air yet? Call it a lie—
moments ago, in a rush to meet my angel,
the one with wings instead of ears,
I took a bite out of my angel's cheek;
it hissed away into the air,
a forgettable sigh. Look,

a curtain has appeared at the window.
Gingerly it lifts, offering these generations
of air. We accept.

I call it linen,
your skin breathing into my ear, this collapse
of air into flesh; its resulting ring,
what we call silence, only shared, touched
with heat, flushed, a little red.

Now we must dismantle our tongues,

something like soft-wrestling
an angel, untying the dock rope.
But we are not a boat, not even an immense, green apple.
We are set free, rising from the bed, adrift now
in these continents of air.

We are constructing this damaged rose
in terms of fire. Fingers,
listen closely to the shadows of your name
as they slide away
—we are not legs anymore, not an ear.

We are a tiny thing, listening closely.

Too big for this room.

THE KISS

I kissed your wrist,
your faintly burning page,
I kissed the sun to sleep—
What a little ocean I hold in my palm,
three stars and a sharp moon, what a little surf
burying itself wave after wave . . .
into coils of concertina wire, they freeze.
I can feel it, if I listen, if I close my eyes,
I can feel it, this breeze lifting its shadow
from the shadow of your hair,
on this coastline of skin anything can happen.
Your lips divide my ribs one by one.
The sun comes and goes with our name
on its lips, my fingers in love with the instant
it takes your breast to be there,
under my tongue. I wanted to believe
I could fold it into my pocket, this vacant lot,
this harvest of baby's breath and broken glass, look,
the sky is touching the sky, O blue vein
buried alive in the neck: my kiss.